The
Seven Secrets
of
Successful Catholics

By
Paul Wilkes

PAULIST PRESS
New York/Mahwah, N.J.

The Publisher gratefully acknowledges use of the following materials: P. 28: Richard P. McBrien, ed., *Catholicism*, New Edition (New York: Harper San Francisco, 1994). P. 40: *Liturgy of the Hours*, vol. 2 (New York: Catholic Book Publishing Co., 1976). P. 41: John Henry Newman, "Essay on the Development of Christian Doctrine"; quoted in John T. Noonan, Jr., "Development in Moral Doctrine," *Theological Studies* 54 (December 1993): 662-67. P. 42: Walter M. Abbott, ed., *The Documents of Vatican II* (New York: Herder and Herder, Association Press, 1966)

A portion of this book appeared in another form in *U.S. Catholic*.

Cover design by Cindy Dunne
Interior design by Joseph E. Petta
Author photo by Marianne Barcellona

Library of Congress Cataloging-in-Publication Data

Wilkes, Paul, 1938–
   The seven secrets of successful Catholics / by Paul Wilkes.
      p.   cm.
   ISBN 0-8091-3795-X (alk. paper)
   1. Christian life–Catholic authors. I. Title.
BX2350.2.W56   1998
248.4′82–dc21   97-51684
                                         CIP

Published by Paulist Press
997 Macarthur Boulevard
Mahwah, New Jersey 07430

Printed and bound in the
United States of America

THE SEVEN SECRETS OF SUCCESSFUL CATHOLICS

Acknowledgments

Many thanks to those good enough to read over my manuscript and both to point out my errors as well as the need for nuance and clarification: Father James Bacik of Corpus Christi University Parish in Toledo, Ohio; Dennis Corcoran, pastoral associate at the Church of the Presentation, Upper Saddle River, New Jersey; MaryKate Codd Davidson, a religious educator in Wilmington, North Carolina; and J. Murray Elwood, a lawyer and scholar in Philadelphia. Special thanks to my excellent editor, Kathleen Walsh.

INTRODUCTION

As I travel about the country talking to Catholics, I find myself continually drawn to a certain kind of Catholic, those who—as Flannery O'Connor put it so well—have what she called a "habit of being."

Men or women, old and young, from all walks of life, cultures and economic strata—there is that special something about them that sets them apart in every group or gathering. It might be an unaffected yet distinctive look in their eyes, the way they speak, a certain presence that they have, or a natural goodness they seem to radiate. They have a certain moral vitality that is both palpable and appealing. And, what is immediately and compellingly apparent is that they seem to really *enjoy* being Catholic.

Their quest is not just to be moral, ethical, or spiritual people—all of which are certainly admirable. It is more than that. They want, expect and rely upon Catholicism to be the motivating force in their lives. Theirs is a Catholic view of life, a Catholic ethos—although I'm sure they might never say such a thing. They simply live it out.

Inevitably I find myself asking them a few basic questions that more or less echo the following: What is it specifically about

Catholicism that works for you? What is it that you do that helps you to live a Catholic life in today's world? Is it difficult for you to live this way? What hints might you give the rest of us? I find that amidst all the diversity and even factiousness in this church of ours there are some striking similarities in their responses.

From those many voices and life experiences, I have distilled what I would like to call *The Seven Secrets of Successful Catholics.*

By "Successful" Catholics, of course, I am not speaking of those who have succeeded in the eyes of the world with regard to job status, academic achievements, the size of their stock portfolios or how big or grand their houses or apartments might be. They are not necessarily the visible leaders in their parish or community. They may be cradle Catholics or converts, the products of years of Catholic education or none at all.

These Catholics are successful because Catholicism is a framework for their beliefs and their actions, a life force at the very center of their beings, a cause both for continuing inspiration and periodic reflection upon who they really are. Catholicism helps them to navigate their way through life; it is a prism through which they view the world. Yes, living a Catholic life can be extraordinarily difficult at times, they would readily admit. But these Catholics have a faith and a practice of that faith that is at once durable and flexible. It is a positive and enriching force.

There is a remarkable paradox in their lives, one that in the eyes of the secular world initially might not make sense. On closer examination it not only makes traditional religious sense, but this paradox also opens them to profound spiritual depth as well as glowing psychological health.

The paradox is this: at the center of Christian—and therefore Catholic—life is the symbol of the cross. The cross means sacrifice, a constant process of dying unto self and being continually reborn. The cross also stands for a monumental manifestation of love.

Living with this paradox certainly means at times being quite unacceptable in the eyes of the world. Denial, not greed. Humility, not pride. Acceptance, not aggression. Forgiveness, not revenge.

Such an approach is exactly the opposite of what success means in the secular world, where objects of material gain or prestige or conquest are eagerly sought; where "going along is getting along."

But the cross and what it represents in human life are eminently practical and too often misunderstood. Sacrifice, discipline, self-denial, deferred gratification are all necessary, when we think about it, for most significant human accomplishments, such as parenthood or physical health. It is no different in a life centered upon common human decency or moral excellence. Successful Catholics, again without saying much about it, have found a rich and fruitful way to live in this paradox. They achieve something far deeper than the success that the world measures.

How strange it is that "success"—so much a term of this world—and Catholicism—which may appear so otherworldly—are so harmoniously joined together for the people who are the inspiration for this book. What makes this union possible, I found, is how they perceive, face and live their Catholicism. For them, Catholicism is not some hair shirt they must begrudgingly wear, or some set of obligations they feel forced to fulfill. Rather than obligations, they see opportunities. They want Catholicism's moral guidelines and sacramental rhythms and yet relish the freedom to think and discern as their Catholic conscience provides. They appreciate Catholicism's rich and ancient traditions, viewing them as having relevance in today's world, and exerting a direct and daily impact on their lives. Catholicism's sacred rituals and sense of community feed both their souls and their human needs. Successful Catholics embrace and relish Catholicism's universal appeal.

They may bridle at Catholicism's demands, but they have found that by living as best they can within a Catholic framework, they

3

have discovered a remarkable fact: they *feel* good when they *are* good. The challenge to greatness embodied in Catholicism is exactly what brings out the best in them. The Catholic path, sometimes narrow and rocky, ultimately takes them where they want to go.

The scriptural passage about the burden being light and the yoke easy might seem like so many idealistic words, but Successful Catholics have found in them their own profound truth. In the divine ecosystem, a life patterned after the precepts that Christ taught and lived works because it makes sense. Although times change–as do their own understanding and perceptions–Successful Catholics have a firm sense of place. They know who they are and where they stand. A Catholic life, properly lived, offers a centeredness they have found nowhere else. A Catholic template provides both ample room and necessary limitations. They are at ease with themselves and with being Catholic.

No, the Successful Catholic's life is not one of solace and certitude. Life itself and life with God are too complex for that. But neither is Catholic life impossible, nor does it merely revolve around a set of abstract codes. It is practical and pragmatic, flexible yet demanding.

Successful Catholics may disagree with the church (most do, on a variety of issues) and many of them have been apart from the church at various times in their lives. But there is something compelling about Catholicism that continually summons them. They may have tried other approaches to God or to personal fulfillment, but none completely satisfied their inner longings. Instead, they exercise the freedom to remain under this wide, sprawling tent of Catholicism, while not always assenting. In our modern day, they are basically saying, "I've searched and searched, Lord, but where can I go? You have the answers, you have the way to true happiness and inner peace. And I've found it here."

It is not that all these Catholics I've met in my travels would look upon themselves as successful in living out all seven of the "secrets." Some of the secrets are ingrained traits or practices; some are goals they yet seek, sturdy threads they want to run through their lives. It is my hope that the secrets might provide room for reflection on whether they are, could be or should be part of your life as a Catholic.

At the end of each chapter, I offer various ways to either enrich that particular secret or to make it your own. These short prayers, reflections and invitations to imagination can be used individually or within a discussion or study group.

Perhaps you have other secrets, equally as important to your Catholic life. At the end of this book I want to offer an opportunity to tell of your experiences with these seven secrets—and to share your own secrets with the rest of us.

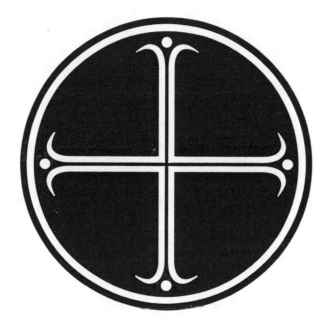

1
SUCCESSFUL CATHOLICS...

Stay close to the eucharist.

The eucharist is both a powerful reality and an unfathomable mystery for Successful Catholics. It is at the very basis of their lives—as people, as Catholics.

Without the eucharist in their lives, they simply feel impoverished, isolated, empty. What a profound moment it is—Successful Catholics told me over and over and in so many different ways—to approach the altar and have an intimate encounter with God. In the midst of public worship they can actually take the body and blood of God's Son into their own beings. Nothing can replace it, this at once so personal yet communal act of intimacy with God. In this profoundly spiritual age, hunger in their souls leads people to seek strength and meaning in so many places, both conventional and bizarre. Here, Successful Catholics know, is the ultimate encounter with the Divine.

It is not that Successful Catholics would not be at home in an ashram or watching whirling dervishes or visiting holy places of other religions. Not that they might not read self-help books that promise fulfillment. But they sense the timeless, unique and so readily available opportunity of the eucharist. They see it as the central fact and sign of Catholic life. Here it is, a gift waiting behind the doors of a tiny chapel on a busy city street or in churches great and small throughout our country. Available to all, no questions asked.

"What I like best about the eucharist is its simplicity," says Jim Helein, a young video producer. "When I return to my pew after receiving, I feel so open, so clear; I can just lay out all the concerns I have and talk to God. I go to a pretty transient parish in Washington D.C., but this is solid, real, unchanging. Nothing transient here. I am in a holy place, regardless of anything else going on around me."

Successful Catholics are hardly some breed apart who are theologically astute and singled out for unique spiritual enlightenment. They continually wrestle with this seemingly incomprehensible mystery, and yet they sense a real presence so palpable, penetrating that very moment in their lives. They somehow, in some way, grasp the reality of Jesus Christ's promise not to abandon his followers and friends, but to continually be present to them in a very real sense until the end of time. When they receive the eucharist, Successful Catholics feel the presence of God in the dailiness and confusion and imperfection of their lives.

These Catholics embody the new spirit alive within the church, a church that has changed in so many ways in our lifetime. Where the eucharist used to be perceived (rightly or wrongly) as a moment when a basically unpleasable God deigned to spend an instant making fleeting contact with one of us wretched sinners, a fuller view of the eucharist is that as much as we hunger to be with God, he hungers to be with us. This is our companion and friend along the journey of life. This is nourishment as continually necessary for the health of our souls as good food sustains our bodies.

And, equally, while the eucharist is certainly extraordinary, it is also *ordinary*, an experience, a moment to which they can return, over and over again. It is as natural—and necessary—as breathing. One morning as I looked out over a weekday mass at a New Jersey suburban parish, I saw a rich mixture of the young and old, men and women, a gathering of the retired, those who work at home, as well as those who have arranged their jobs so they could be there.

Stay close to the eucharist.

While others in their town are out on the golf course or jogging, at the desk or sink or computer station, this is a priority for them; this is the way they choose to begin their day. They wouldn't have it any other way.

In Many Ways

The reception of the eucharist is a spiritual feast set within the larger feast of the liturgy that Successful Catholics have found offers them unique encounters with God. A liturgical renewal has swept through the church, transforming what was once viewed as an obligation to be performed into a rich opportunity for holiness. Successful Catholics have resonated to the genius of liturgical renewal that has transformed worship and Catholic understanding of how God might be made present to them. No longer is it a case of a priest "saying" mass before a passive audience. Liturgy is the prayer of the church, *their* church, *them.*

The readings from scripture are not merely the recitation of ancient words, but Christ being present to his church in that very moment. "I need to hear those words every week," says Beata Welsh, a transportation consultant and mother, "and when I listen I always find something that speaks directly to my life. I can almost hear Christ talking to me, helping me work through those things that are on my mind."

Successful Catholics like Beata also realize that the community around her itself expresses the presence of God. These, the "eucharistic people," as Catholics are well named, believe literally that "where two or more of you are gathered in my name, I am with you." As Christ gathered others around in his life to face the challenges that God placed before him, so does the community pause on life's journey to come together and invite him once more into their midst.

Not a Matter of Deserving

It is not that Successful Catholics look upon themselves as especially deserving of the eucharist, or that they receive the eucharist casually. Successful Catholics are well aware of their faults, at times utterly frustrated with themselves that they are not better people. They have so many good intentions and yet they often come to the altar hardly models of proper Catholic behavior. But their awareness of their unworthiness is not an ever-deepening spiral of self-accusation and despair. They are not people who believe that you have to be perfect to receive our Lord. They aspire to be perfect, but they understand their own humanity.

They look upon the eucharist as an invitation for God to do for them what they cannot always do for themselves. They want to be made whole, made clean, sanctified. They are humbled and heartened by the invitation, to "take, eat," and heartened by those simple words that come just before the eucharist is distributed: "Lord, I am not worthy to receive you, but only say the word and I shall be healed." They believe keenly that their sins are forgiven and forgotten, and that they will be healed, strengthened, sustained. Whether they need insight to make a tough decision or just the endurance to live out another day in a difficult situation, they look to the eucharist to provide it.

The desire to be close to God, they know, sends a message of love that a heavenly Father will not spurn. Prodigals they may be, but they are assured of being welcomed home and having a feast spread out before them. "I'm from the old church, which emphasized the pious ways of bowing your head and worshipping in silence, afraid that you weren't going to say the right words and God would be angry at you," says Mary Anne Barry, a retired social worker and grandmother. "But now when I receive, I have this feeling of a good and compassionate God who wants the best for me. This isn't some ritualistic formality; it's about a relationship between a God who wants to be in my life and all I have to do is say 'Yes, come in.'"

Ever Deepening Understanding

As Successful Catholics have added years to their lives, so have they added understanding and a growing appreciation of the eucharist. Yes, for many their first communion day is one that they will always treasure, but Successful Catholics do not remain in the past, hoping that fond memories can somehow provide the spiritual sustenance for a lifetime. They have different needs; their lives have taken some amazing twists and turns. They need God here, today, present to them. Many of them have been away from the church at various times in their lives, but it was the eucharist as much as anything else that brought them back. With the eucharist there was that wonderful feeling of being home, of being made whole once again. They received the eucharist in thanks when their lives were going well and in utter desperation when hope seemed a foolish word. Indeed, it has been the sacrament for all the seasons of their lives.

"The mass is not a performance; it is a gathering of people with their struggles, their disagreements, their pains, their triumphs," says Pat Reardon, a newspaper reporter. "We're not out to homogenize people and somehow make them all the same. No, there we are in all our uncomfortable diversity, before God, ready to ask him to come into our midst, as messy as it is—but that's all we have. That's us!"

Receiving the eucharist provides not only a sacred encounter that is to be treasured but is, as Numa Torres, the father of two children

13

and an emigrant from El Salvador, understands it, a continuing force for our lives. The eucharist is not something that exists only in church, but whose magic and mystery go out into the streets. "When I take the bread to share, it is a sign to me that I must share my talents and my values, my material things with people around me," he says. "Christ shared; I must share."

So the eucharist is not only a private moment with God, but food and inspiration to take into the day, into the week. "I need to refocus on the dream," says Dick Westly, a college professor. "And that dream is to transform the world into a fitting place for people and for God. It's that simple." Successful Catholics understand that when they "do this in memory of me," they are doing it ritually in church and really in their own lives.

Each Has Different Needs

The eucharist is a powerful symbol for Successful Catholics, a vivid, tactile—and reassuring—reminder of the vast community of which they are a part. As they join the line slowly moving toward the altar, there is an abiding sense of community that they seldom feel with this intensity. Each person approaches the altar with his or her own needs, own thoughts, own prayers—articulated or not. We come forward in good times and in bad. Jesus beckons to us when we walk upright or when our lives weigh heavily upon our shoulders. Here, Catholics are not distinguished by their fervor or depth of belief or state in life; they are all equal before God. In fact, they may have very different meanings of what the eucharist actually is. All around the world, other Catholics, rich and poor, holy and sinful, are approaching other altars, all seeking to encounter God.

It is not that Successful Catholics haven't gone to other places for spiritual sustenance—they have, they do and they will. "I love the peacefulness of a Quaker meeting when I go," says Marty Hegarty, an organizational consultant, "but I need the living sign of God's presence that the eucharist is to me."

The eucharist is a visible sign of the unity and strength of Catholicism, and it is a statement of an utter need as Catholics—a need that is met so poignantly in that tiny, tasteless wafer and perhaps a sip of not-so-good wine. Successful Catholics talk unabashedly of their hunger for this spiritual food and how, once received, a sense of calm and peace and power comes over them. Successful Catholics realize they are having an encounter with the divine. In that moment lies the opportunity to experience God in a way different from any other. Successful Catholics treasure those eucharistic moments.

Further Thought and Action

Reflection

The God who created you and everything on this earth is available in the eucharist. This is a loving God, not a bookkeeper, a caring father who seeks always your true happiness. In the eucharist, and within a community, you have the opportunity to encounter at once the God of the ages, who will enlighten and direct you—an "abba," daddy, a loving father whose arms are open to you. He wants to be with you.

Words to Ponder:

"Take this, all of you, and eat, for this is my body."

Just Imagine... *

...yourself walking down a side street in Jerusalem some two thousand years ago. The street is dark. You see up ahead light streaming out from a doorway. Inside Jesus and his friends have gathered for the last supper. They beckon you to come in and sit with them for this meal. You enter. You say nothing. You listen to the voices of this man and his friends.

He pauses during the meal and says he wants to share himself in a special way with those gathered around him this night—and every time his followers gather together in his name. You may not be quite sure who he is, or what his message of love and forgiveness and self-acceptance really means, but there is something in his face, his presence that is so comforting, so appealing. A loaf of bread is passed, each person breaking off a piece to eat. The loaf is passed to you.

Questions to Ponder:

✚ How is it that God can actually be present in the eucharist? What does that mean to me?

✚ What was my first belief about the eucharist? How do I understand it now?

✚ How do I take the eucharist into my life?

---

* Put yourself in the situation offered in "Just imagine..." in each chapter. Use your senses fully; put no bounds on your imagination. Walk, rest, listen. Talk to the people you meet and see. Experience this moment as vividly as you can.

Stay close to the eucharist.

A Prayer

"Lord, I want so badly to be close to you, to know your wishes for my life, to feel the power that you alone can give me to live a decent and meaningful life. Let me feel your presence in a new way, not restrained by my doubts or confusion, but unleashed by that clarity of vision that you—and you alone—can give me. Help me to take that presence into my daily life, in what I do or say or even what I think."

If It Is Not Yet Yours, Making This Secret Your Own

Plan how and where you will receive the eucharist. Think of it as a "first communion." It may be in the company of many at a Sunday morning mass or with few at a weekday mass near where you work or live. Or, you might have a special church—the church of your baptism or marriage, a small chapel, the church at a monastery or retreat house. Think about that eucharist in the hours and days before you receive it. God will be with you, God wants to be with you. Soon this will happen.

Allow the power of the eucharist to sweep over you once you have received. God is with you. You may wish to remain silent or to speak to him, for he is physically present within you. Tell him about yourself, your life, your concerns. You are encountering the person with the power to transform you, to give you the insight; the strength you need is at hand. Feel that power. Pause and listen.

If It Already Is,
A Way to Deepen the Secret

The next time you rise up from your pew to receive the eucharist, bring to the altar the part of your life—a problem, a person, a situation, a sorrow, a bad habit—that is your greatest burden. As you reach out your hands for the eucharist, place that burden before God. In return he gives you himself. As you return to the pew, sit quietly and meditate on this mystical exchange.

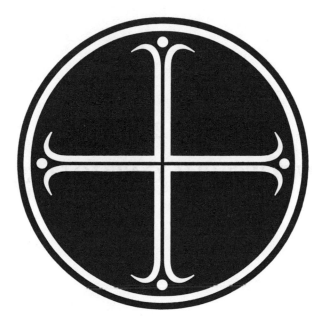

2
SUCCESSFUL CATHOLICS...

Are members of a faith community.

Successful Catholics have found they need the company of others on their journeys toward God. They need a home for the spirit. Individuals though they certainly are, they need companions along the way.

Many Successful Catholics have, at one time or another, cut themselves off from a faith community, choosing to go it alone, sometimes rationalizing that they could be just as close to God by themselves as with a group of people. In certain ways they were right. God comes to us in silence, in prayer, in an inspirational book, in the events of our day. We need not be in a church to experience God's presence. But Successful Catholics felt a reoccurring need to be part of a larger community so that they might be reminded that they are not alone, they are not strange creatures going about some impossible task. They acknowledge that they are social beings who need to provide and receive reinforcement from others who—while they may have different spiritual goals and concepts—want to be in the presence of those who have similar ideals.

"I need a vote of confidence that I'm trying to do a good job at work, raise my children well, make sense out of my life," says Tom Lenz, an urban planner. "Just being with the people in my parish every Sunday—not an affluent parish, ethnically diverse, yet composed of people admitting we need help—makes me feel that I'm not in this alone."

Joan Sullivan, an unmarried woman who decided to become a foster mother, had been away from the church for a long time, but when she found herself "the head of this family of goofy teenagers, I remembered my own parents' model of parish life. I wanted to give the kids a sense of moral life, of community life, of stability. The parish was perfect, and it became part of our extended family."

The Search

As many Successful Catholics have discovered, however, the closest parish was not always the right place for them. "A spiritual home is too important a part of people's lives to leave to chance or to their address," says Father Jack Wall, who revived downtown Chicago's once moribund Old Saint Patrick's into a vibrant, active parish. "We have 350 couples involved in mixed marriages, we have hard-driving corporate executives, we have people hungry for a substantial spiritual life who just are not going to settle for pablum. People with unique yet common needs. And many of them told us this was their last stop. They were tired of looking and being disappointed. If they didn't find a church home here, their search was over. Parishes that listen to people's faith stories and struggles are parishes that are overflowing, and there are plenty of good parishes out there—if you care enough, you'll find one."

Successful Catholics know well what Father Wall is talking about. Many of them searched and searched for a parish that would speak to their souls as well as their minds and hearts, that would excite them with Catholicism's message and challenge them to be the people they knew they wanted to be. I received a letter from an elderly couple who had been in a dynamic New Jersey parish but

Are members of a faith community.

were now despairing that their children, spread out from coast to coast, could not find similarly wonderful spiritual homes. Successful Catholics are sometimes lucky to have such a parish nearby, but if they are not so lucky, then they must be persistent. By visiting various parishes, becoming part of the Catholic grapevine and simply by asking Catholics whom they admire, they can usually find their place.

A recent Notre Dame study indicated that fully seventy-five percent of American Catholics do not attend mass each week. Yes, this may be testimony to the fact that ours are busy lives, that obligation and guilt no longer motivate and, moreover, that not enough parishes are alive and appealing. But perhaps it is also a statement that too many Catholics have forgotten (or have not yet discovered) the central place in their spiritual life that a good parish can occupy.

Other Faith Communities

For many Successful Catholics, like Tom Lenz and Joan Sullivan, their spiritual home and faith community is the traditional parish, but for others it may be a Newman Center on a college campus, a Catholic Worker house in the inner city, a small Christian or base community, a Cursillo or a Bible study group. Lay associations that link themselves to specific monastic communities are another example of those who have voluntarily taken on a more disciplined prayer life. Worship and community can revolve around a quiet mass with the Trappists, in a swirling group of kids and adults at a folk mass housed in a gym, or in a prayer group gathered around a coffee table in someone's living room. Whatever its form, a faith community provides both a secure and recognizable home for the spirit and that wellspring of graces promised to the first followers of Christ—and to us in our day. Faith communities that both gather regularly and reach out readily—history continually instructs us—simply work. Where two or more are gathered, indeed, the spirit is present in a special way.

Successful Catholics have come to these faith communities in a variety of ways. Some found that parish life and large corporate worship in a weekly liturgy did not meet all their spiritual needs. Still others came upon a faith community by accident or through a friend—often at a time of intense searching, personal pain or transition in their lives. But what is characteristic of the best faith communities is that virtually all of them maintain strong ties to a parish and the larger church. Successful Catholics who are members of prayer groups and small communities that have been in existence for as long as twenty-five or thirty years are inevitably also parish members. Small groups can begin to construct their own journey to the truth, and Successful Catholics, while charting their individual paths to God, still see themselves as part of the universal church.

If there is a visible growing edge to the church, it is in these small groups that are cropping up all over the country. What the Successful Catholics involved in these groups are saying is that they want both the focus and the personal accountability afforded by smaller groupings of people. In essence, they aspire to a more intense and personal community of believers who participate in activities that complement their parish affiliation without replacing it.

Family Stories, Faith Stories

The most alive and faith-filled American parishes (and those, incidentally, with more than their share of Successful Catholics) are often the parishes that encourage the telling of individuals' faith stories through retreats or small group encounters. As they sit in the pews (or at home on Sunday morning), too many Catholics feel they are the only ones who have a hard time being moral in an immoral world, who feel a flatness in their spiritual lives, who have difficulties putting family, work and leisure in proper perspective. To hear others wrestling with the same issues is to realize that life presents a set of difficulties for each person. It is how those difficulties are viewed and approached that makes all the difference. The burden does become lighter—and the triumph greater—when it is shared.

Successful Catholics choose their parish for many reasons. Some are drawn to the majesty of great liturgy and music, others to a place involved in effective social ministry, insightful religious education or great youth programs. The attractions of parishes and faith communities are as diverse as the people who compose them. "But I wouldn't search around for the one-hundred percent perfect parish," warns John Fialka, an investigative reporter. "It doesn't exist. Find a reasonably good one that makes sense to you and work within it; that's the key."

The parish is not a place that requires perfection of those who participate in its life. It is a place to grow, a community, a family really. And, like any family, the parish can be unwieldy at times. In families and in parishes there is that rich composite: members who brighten the room and those not always so marvelous. "Just because you have a difficult uncle or a mother you fight with, that doesn't cause you to abandon your family," says Marty Hegarty. "And anyhow the parish *is* the church," says Leon Roberts, a musician, "a place where there are no pretenses, where Christ strips you down to your very essence, where you are held accountable—and yet it is a massive support group that stands with you."

In Good Season, in All Seasons

Parishes are certainly there for Successful Catholics in their happiest moments—after all, where else do Catholics go to celebrate the most significant times in their lives—birth and death, the reception of the first spiritual food, acceptance into adulthood, marriage? Of course, it is the parish. Successful Catholics cherish those signal events, but these do not provide the opportunity to gather and address the needs that each week brings. "The parish was there for me when I was going through the most difficult times in my marriage," says a Washington, D.C. woman. "That couldn't be taken away from me when everything else was crumbling. This was my family, and they didn't run away at the worst time of my life." And for Mary Murphy Zastrow, a kindergarten aide, who disagreed bitterly with the church and found herself at its margins, "My children receiving the sacraments at the parish drew me back in; I learned with them. And the pastor wouldn't let me go; I just got drawn back in, even with all my ambivalence. I realized this was still my home; I wanted to be there."

Successful Catholics are people who come to their parishes to hear the family stories of their ancestors. They want to be amazed and enlightened, shocked and consoled by the words of scripture that speak to them so poignantly each week. The ancient stories are made new in our day, in the circumstances of our lives. The church cycle of readings intersects with our life cycles, beaming distant, true light into our darkest corners.

And Successful Catholics are people who want to pass along their own stories of what it is to live a Catholic life today. This is an important tradition to them. They have this innate sense that they are in a long line of Catholics, stretching back to Christ and extending far beyond the limits of their imagination. Parishes and faith communities provide an oasis for the gathering of their particular clans, each on a different pilgrimage, but all seeking to know and be close to God. Successful Catholics want to be prodded; they want to be encouraged; they want to be fed. They realize that Catholicism is not some obscure, abstract way of life; it needs specific places where it is taught and where the attempt is made to begin to live its precepts and promises. "In parishes, we all need to be present to each other so then we can go out into the world and not just talk the talk, but walk the walk," says Allen Stryczek, a business systems consultant.

With all its imperfections, that parish or monastery or prayer group is their faith family of the present. Can they visualize better groups to be with, more appropriate and holier places to be? Maybe. But, in reality, this is their family, with all its majesty and short-comings. This is their reunion, filled with laughter and tears. As they search other faces, it is soon clear that many may share their ambivalence, but they too have made this commitment. If not these *exact* words, then certainly this sentiment echoes their inner voices: "We are here, Lord, gathered together, struggling to know you and to lead a better life. We want to be close to you, to understand you. We need your help. Help us. Feed us."

A Hub, a Center

Successful Catholics, as part of a parish, are finding again that it can be an important center for their lives. It is not that Successful Catholics are at their parish every day or involved in a myriad of its activities. But the ideals that the parish stands for radiate out into their lives, into the community. Being considered a member of a certain parish is its own statement about that person. It is here that concern for others and kindness and honesty are the coin of the realm, for this is a place that testifies "...to values which other-wise might be forgotten and lost, to the detriment of the human community itself," as the authoritative book *Catholicism* states (p. 730). It is in the parish that a sense of service to others is inculcated in children. Imperfect it may be, and its pews filled with imperfect people, the parish is still a beacon on the hill. What other place in our lives has as its primary goal to make us holy and bring us closer to God?

A synergism and connectedness result. Being involved in a parish naturally draws Catholics to other Catholics and Catholic institutions. The retired have found the parish a perfect place to express their goodness, now that they have more time available. Generation X, mobile families, the single and divorced, all are quickly able to sink roots into a community through a parish.

Successful Catholics make conscious choices about parish life—they support Catholic schools, they try to be part of Catholic events, from dances to baseball games. Not that they are ghetto Catholics, or only socialize with Catholics, but they like to be in the company of other Catholics. There is a common language and folklore, a centeredness. Indeed, "Catholic" is still spoken here.

Further Thought and Action

Reflection

The support and presence of other people has always been a key element in Catholic life. It was in groups—not individually—that the earliest Christians learned of the ways of Jesus, fostered those beliefs, and received encouragement to go on. Jesus himself sought others to be with, both to begin to live the way of God and for support during his days on earth. We are social beings; we need to know we are not alone in our pursuits; we need to be in the company of others who share our vision. God has told us that he is present in our gathering together—so these moments are blessed. We want others to share in our triumphs and moments of grace. We need their help when we are weak. And, in helping the weak ourselves, we become stronger, more confident.

Words to Ponder

"Where two or more are gathered together in my name, I am with you."

Just Imagine...

...you have been invited to supper at a most unlikely place, the home of a Roman tax collector. This is a hated person, an oppressor of your people. You find that Jesus has also been invited, so your curiosity wins out and you go. You watch as Jesus and the tax collector talk. You are amazed that Jesus does not condemn him for what he does, but asks that he be honest in his work. You look around the room. Who else is there in this gathering of those who want to be close to Jesus and to hear his words? Merchants, slaves, men, women—those who publicly practice their faith and those who do not. Is it right for them to be here with Jesus? For you? For the tax collector? Jesus is saying something. "Love one another as I have loved you." What does he mean by that?

Questions to Ponder:

✛ Do I really need a home for my spiritual life or have I been successful "going it alone"?

✛ Reflecting back over my life, in what parish setting have I felt most at home? What was it that made me feel most welcome there?

✛ What happens to me in the midst of a group of people who, while different, have similar goals? What happens to me when they espouse similar goals, but have very different ways of achieving them?

A Prayer

"Lord, I want to be close to you and understand your message for my life. But I cannot do this alone. I know I already have your help. You have always been there, even when I tried to shut you out. Now help me find other Catholic companions along the way of life. Lead me to that community of faith in which I can serve and in which I will find refuge and strength."

If Not Yet Yours, Making This Secret Your Own

If you seek a home for your spirit, give the parish a chance. You may be hesitant, but ask Catholic friends what they like best about parishes in your area—and then visit them. When you are there, look in the bulletin for what the parish does and stands for. As you sit in the pews, try to hear the others' voices calling out to God; let your own request be heard in the stillness of this place. Be open. Be quiet. Listen to God's word and wisdom for your life. Don't be shy about

Are members of a faith community.

introducing yourself to people around you, to the priest after mass. Make an appointment to talk to the priest about the parish.

If It Already Is,
A Way to Deepen the Secret

Share a story about your spiritual home with somebody within the coming week. There are people all around you looking for a home for their spirit—newcomers, parents with children, searchers, those who seem not to have a center to their lives. Tell that person what your own spiritual home means to you and why it is so important in your life.

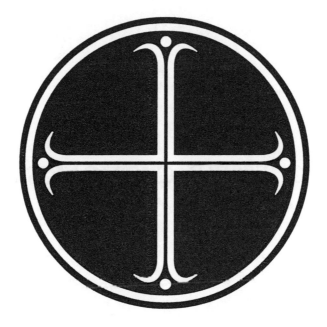

3

SUCCESSFUL CATHOLICS...

Rely on their conscience
and good judgement—
but never alone.

Successful Catholics may or may not have heard of Cardinal John Henry Newman, may or may not know of his wisdom and teachings—but they are surely his heirs. For, before there was a Vatican II, there was Newman, an Anglican turned Catholic, eventually elevated to Cardinal, who loved the church enough to tell it that there were even higher powers in his life. For it was Newman who best articulated the crucial place individual conscience played in the development and practice of moral character. Newman called conscience "the kindly light" that would illuminate our minds to make sound, moral decisions.

And it was Vatican II—some hundred years later and standing on Newman's shoulders—that told a Catholic world which had been discouraged from making personal decisions on both simple and complex moral issues that their individual consciences were to be the supreme arbiter of their actions. Vatican II informed Catholics of amazing new powers and rights—and the equally serious responsibilities that came with them. Yes, there would always be rules and regulations, doctrine and dogma, but ultimately nothing ranked above that mysterious thing called a conscience.

Successful Catholics have accepted that awesome challenge. Not with arrogance, or because they seek easy ways to rationalize their actions, but with a certain humility that comes from realizing a great trust has been placed in them—and they are quietly confident that such trust is deserved. Successful Catholics, confronted by the many moral decisions they have to make each day, now realize that they carry within themselves the ability to make good decisions. Their conscience, their instincts, their sense of fairness and decency—and their common sense—stand ready to address even the most complex and most difficult decisions they will have to make.

But Successful Catholics are not so undiscerning as to think that their conscience can be formed or exercised in a vacuum. Catholics are called to "put on the mind of Christ" in exercising their conscience. And this is what Successful Catholics attempt to do, to look to the doctrine, tradition and norms of their church—yet not to be hamstrung or overwhelmed by myriad rules and regulations. Different situations call for different responses and the informed conscience of a Successful Catholic is ready to interpret, even right on the spot, what decision to make and what direction to take. Successful Catholics aspire not merely to factual, dogmatic adherence to Catholic teaching (the letter of the law), but ultimately to truth and justice (the spirit of the law).

"God didn't make us simply to adhere to a set of rules," says Lena Shipley, a religious education teacher. "His Son came to reveal a 'higher' road, the way of divine love. I always go back to the story of the rich young man in scripture. He kept all the commandments—the letter of the law—but Jesus asked him for something more than that: to give himself away. He couldn't do it and he went away sadly. To me, the letter of the law is helpful, but it is not an end in itself. This is the world of the mind, a means to an end, which is a life lived according to that spirit of the law."

Rely on their conscience and good judgement—but never alone.

Underpinnings

There was a day, not that long ago, when to be considered a *good* Catholic was to be a Catholic who meticulously followed all the rules, participated in the proper rituals on the proper day and in the proper place, and looked to the church—almost like an infant constantly looking to a parent—to make their decisions. It was not that this was wrong, but it was a stage of development within Catholicism—this dynamic, changing, ever self-evaluating body of believers, with the Holy Spirit ever present in the process. Successful Catholics have now grown up, ready to be treated and to act as adults. And God continues to be with them.

This is an exciting challenge to be sure, to be—in essence—our own moral agents. But it is hardly easy to live a Catholic, moral life that puts so much responsibility upon individual conscience. Making sound decisions is often extraordinarily difficult, and one's conscience can be terribly conflicted and confused about what is really the best course of action. Successful Catholics admit that sometimes they would like to have more black and white in their lives, more clear choices.

The death penalty, marriage and divorce, abortion, overpopulation, women's rights, human rights, raising children. The list goes on. Where to draw the line?

But, equally, Successful Catholics have come to realize they have within them the innate ability to make good—if not always right—decisions. They know they do not have to construct a value system each day, for their consciences are built not upon their moods or emotions, the whims of the day, or the changing sands of popular culture, but upon centuries of church tradition and teaching. They are solidly grounded in the wisdom, the decency and the practicality of the Judeo-Christian ethic. They are continually refreshed and informed by an ever-growing body of Catholic social teachings. Successful Catholics look to their church and their God, as well as their families, parents and elders, their Catholic education, the other formative people in their lives–and themselves–all forging a moral and resilient partnership. They understand that God stands with them in the many confusing and seemingly morally impossible situations that life presents; they are not and will never be alone.

Forget that there are conflicting opinions about basic human values and conduct throughout our society–Successful Catholics acknowledge that while espousing Catholic principles, two priests, two bishops, even two popes might come down very differently on crucial issues. So there is a certain *inevitability* that conscience would have to play a pivotal role in their lives. While imperfect, it is still the best moral compass they have. And it is always with them. They hope (and pray) that it is well formed; they constantly try to improve their own abilities to make sound moral judgements by being open to new events, new insights and the ever mysterious force of the Holy Spirit.

But Successful Catholics are also careful not to use their conscience as a convenient excuse to do what they want to do rather than what they know they should do. They do not reach decisions in life based on convenience or expediency. They realize that conscience is not merely a feeling, but a complex combination of intuition, knowledge and awareness of the actual situation.

A New Openness

With their conscience as their guide, Successful Catholics find that they need not be frightened by the many voices calling out to them, the confusing messages, both secular and religious, the threats of damnation for believing this or the promise of eternal reward for advocating that. They can be open to other points of view that may not agree with theirs. Yes, they have firm ideas on what their Catholic life should be about. They may be adamant that the clergy should remain celibate and male; they may differ with the church's teachings on birth control or on the ability of the divorced and remarried to receive the eucharist. Today's Catholics are not what they were a generation ago, when strict, exact guidelines covered so many aspects of their lives and left little room for personal interpretation.

Today's Successful Catholics realize the constant need to be challenged and to be tempered, to hear the points of view of others—whether this is comfortable or not. They realize that as strong as their opinions are, they might need to be altered or even reversed. They understand the need to constantly reinform their conscience. This does not mean that Successful Catholics continually waffle on the big issues of the day. For the most part, they do not. But they sense that being open to other opinions is not a sign of weak convictions, but of convictions that are strong enough to stand up to questioning. Their lives mirror the sentiments of Saint Peter Damian when he said, "Stand in justice and fear. Prepare your soul; it is about to be tested."

For conscience is not static. True moral maturity is arrived at (if ever) through a constant process of evolution. Some of the blinding insights or beliefs of our youth simply don't stand up under the weight of the years and other experiences. Likewise, our conscience is constantly being formed and reformed. The proper understanding of conscience and how to properly utilize this "kindly light" is a revelation that comes to Successful Catholics at various times in their lives.

"I had always understood that conscience was the proximate internal form of morality," says J. Murray Elwood, a lawyer and an expert on Cardinal Newman, "but I never felt easy taking responsibility for my major ethical decisions. I'd run to my confessor for affirmation in some choices and back off on others. Then one day at mass I heard that parable about the landowner giving his servants a certain amount of money, saying, 'Trade until I come.' It hit me! The Lord leaves me here in this life with my intelligence, my Catholic education, my talents, my basic ethical sense, and he isn't so concerned that I always bat a thousand in my choices. He trusts me enough to run a risk."

Here is another way to say it: "We are in a sense our own parents, and we give birth to ourselves by our own free choice of what is good." To some that might sound like the equivocating utterance of a New Age prophet. Actually these are the words of Saint Gregory of Nyssa (*Breviary* III, page 238), a fourth-century bishop and theologian who had very firm ideas on what conscience was all about. Gregory profoundly sensed the crucial role of spiritual and moral maturity in a person's development.

"At one time in my life, being an angry black man made complete sense to me," says Hal Gordon, an intercity community organizer. "Hate, rage—hey, I had every reason to be angry at what happened to my people. I felt great about it. For a while. Gradually, my conscience kept working on me and I eventually saw that unless I turned my rage into a positive force, it just didn't make any sense. But, believe me, it took a while."

Or as Chris Zurawsky, a young medical editor, has found it to be: "When I feel remorse, when I feel downright crummy, I know I've violated my conscience. Sometimes I can kid myself, but not for long. It always catches up with me." Successful Catholics have this sixth sense—feeling either "crummy" or comfortable about their decisions. They know that God judges them, not by what they actually do or don't do, but by what they have in their hearts.

To Change

The Successful Catholic looks out over this vast tent under which a billion people find their shelter. Under that tent will be people whose conclusions, lifestyles and very personalities are diametrically in opposition with their own. Are they lesser Catholics? What of the so-called "cafeteria Catholics," or unswervingly traditionalistic Catholics? Does God love them less?

The Successful Catholic realizes that life is a pilgrimage and not a prepackaged trip. The winds of history will blow as they will and conditions will change dramatically. Successful Catholics look back upon their lives, complete with all the many twists and turns, and realize that the points of view they now vehemently disagree with were often the very ones they once held. Such reflections bring with them not only a sense of charity, but a sense of humor as well.

As the morally righteous wag fingers at them for their ability to change, for their readiness to admit that they were wrong in their judgement and now must act in another way, Successful Catholics hearken back to the "kindly light," Newman's concept of the conscience. "Here below to live is to change," he said. "And to be perfect is to have changed often." (Essay on the Development of Christian Doctrine)

Further Thought and Action

Reflection

God is not only a loving God, but a trusting God. He did not make us in his image to have us slavishly and unthinkingly follow a long list of preordained rules. He endowed us with the tools to make good judgements—our intellect and our natural instinct for good, the teachings of the church, the moral example of others and our insights into the changing world around us. Through prayer we can bring God's insights into our lives. All these form our conscience—and, properly formed and used, it is the best guide for our lives.

Just Imagine...

...you are sitting in the shade of a leafy fig tree with Jesus. All the others are at some distance, so you are alone with him for the moment. You find yourself telling him of a situation in your life about which you are having a very difficult time making a decision, not knowing what to do or how to act. You go into some detail and it seems the situation is even more complicated than you imagined. There seems no "right" way and certainly no easy answer. You finish and await his advice.

"Let us pray together for a moment," is the response. "I know you will make the right decision and I stand with you on it. I trust *you*."

You look at him. And he looks at you.

Words to Ponder:

"Deep within his conscience man discovers a law which he has not laid upon himself but which he must obey. Its voice, ever calling him to love and to do what is good and to avoid evil, sounds in his heart at the right moment" (*Gaudium et Spes* 16 [Vatican II]).

Questions to Ponder

✤ Why is it that my individual conscience is the best moral guide I will ever have? What makes me doubt that I can make good decisions, relying on my informed conscience?

✤ When have I convinced myself that I was following my conscience, but really only wanted to act in a certain way? Had I "informed" my conscience sufficiently?

✤ When in my life, after prayer and thought, have I followed my own conscience in a difficult ethical choice?

A Prayer

"Lord, my knowledge of the world—and of myself—is so limited. So often it is hard for me to make sound moral judgements. I doubt myself. But I believe that because you love me and because you are always with me, you gave me this wondrous capability and trust me to use it well. Because, like your presence, my conscience I always have with me. Enlighten my mind and my conscience so that I can make bold, good judgements in which both of us can take pride."

If Not Yet Yours, Making This Secret Your Own

Although you may doubt your ability—and the good instincts of your conscience—go out into this day and give your conscience the opportunity to prove itself. When you are confronted with a difficult situation or decision, don't shy away from it, but let your conscience help you make the decision for you. Allow not only your formal church train-

ing, but the good examples of people you admire to be on your mind as you try to figure out what to do. Pray for guidance. Look upon yourself as a person who is trying to live a moral life by seeking to do what is right. In good conscience, act.

If It Already Is,
A Way to Deepen the Secret

Reflect on a time in your life when your conscience dictated that you change your mind and actions on a particular issue or person or circumstance. Go through your reasoning in both situations, concentrating on what had changed to make *you* change. What was it that set you apart from other people in this matter? Was there any element of self-righteousness in either decision?

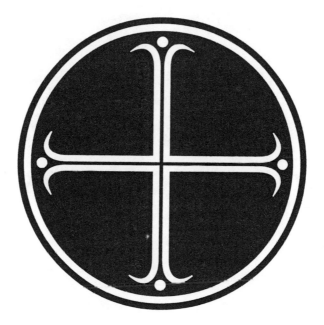

4

SUCCESSFUL CATHOLICS...

Regularly do things that call them out of themselves.

It has become a common and easy complaint for people of our time to rail against an unkind and unjust world, to point out how society seems to be deteriorating. Surely we all see examples every day. Successful Catholics are hardly immune from such an attitude, but they are able to see opportunities for holiness and wholeness in the midst of sometimes very troubling circumstances. Privately—in small actions no one will ever know of—and publicly—taking on larger social issues—Successful Catholics go about making this world a better place. For their own sanity, to maintain a sense of decency and, quite honestly, to preserve the very essence of what it is to be Catholic, they simply find that they have no other choice. In order to live the Catholic tradition that comes down from the time of the apostles to our very day, Successful Catholics find that they must practice what is preached to them.

Whether it be running for the school board, fighting for a shelter for the homeless or confronting someone or something that denies people their dignity, Successful Catholics are people who absolutely must do things that call them out of themselves. For them it is a normal practice or "habit of being," usually done consciously, but oftentimes unconsciously. They realize that Catholicism without practical application withers like an unwatered plant.

Successful Catholics take seriously their baptismal mandate to be priest, prophet and king. Good works, simple or great, serve to revitalize their Catholic faith, illustrate its practical application and provide the doers with that deep, abiding sense that they are called not only to know or talk about—but to express—Christ's way in their daily lives.

And, as these Successful Catholics go about these deeds, they experience not so much a sense of sacrifice as of completeness. Doing good things for other people gives them pleasure. It adds to their lives. It does not subtract. They are not less for having seen a need and trying their best to meet it, but more. And, thus encouraged, they want to do still more. They see themselves as cocreators of this world with God. If they don't do it, who will?

At the core of Successful Catholics is a generosity of spirit, a certain eagerness and ability to make life better, fuller for other people. I recall meeting Father Joseph Greer, a priest in Natick, Massachusetts who I eventually wrote about a few years ago. He was a man who got enormous enjoyment from helping people. On the surface, he could be gruff, impatient, stubborn at times, yet when the opportunity to pick up the phone to make sure a kid got into college, a struggling family received the rent money they needed, or a fellow priest the assignment he coveted, Father Greer was ready to help. He got a kick out of being the person who could make a difference; it was a challenge for him to see if *this* time, *each* time, he could make it happen.

My own father—a hardworking carpenter who never preached one syllable about how to live a Catholic life—had a simple piece of advice for his seven children: do one unasked for, unrewarded thing a day. It took me many years to see the wisdom and the depth of his example. Successful Catholics live by a similar code, however they might put it into words—and action. Small deeds, random acts of kindness have an amazing ability to transform the most ordinary experiences of our day.

Angels in the Flesh

Much has been said and written about angels over the past decade, but Successful Catholics—and again, they would never allow anyone to say this about them—are actually angels in the flesh. They are people who grant that, while divine power and divine intervention are fine and that celestial creatures may have their role in our lives, caring human acts are always within our capabilities. Instead of waiting for angels to visit, Successful Catholics act.

So much of the current fascination with crystals, horoscopes, channeling and all kinds of supposed spiritual intercessors has a certain passive quality about it—a no-work, no-risk path to enlightenment and happiness. It's as if this life were to be the result of some sort of magic, or a cosmic chess game that we can only observe and not influence. Well, Successful Catholics are people who *bring about* transcendent moments with completely human actions, often taking chances that they will be misunderstood or regarded as fools. They are continually willing to make an effort to see God in other people. They are willing to puzzle. Others may not understand them, but they know so deeply in their very beings how necessary is this outpouring of themselves.

Matt Doyle, a North Carolina friend of mine, and a single father who is raising his two children, sees it this way: "I wonder if it's about grand gestures or if it happens almost without notice. When we follow the mandates of the Sermon on the Mount, there is nothing grand there. Most of what is called for is simple and easy and often neglected. When we give the guy on the street the quarter, when we take time to give someone directions when we are in a hurry, when we listen to someone's boring story about something that is deeply important to them, when we don't react with anger even when it is justified. These are the times we are called out—not when we chair the campaign for something or other; not when we offer to serve on the parish councils and committees. While all those are important, they are not so important as the little moments of greatness that present themselves every day."

The Catholic way of life has always been built upon a firm foundation of communal morality, not rugged individualism; it espouses interdependence, not a hands-off, at-a-distance independence that false prophets in our time—and those through the ages—have preached. In early Christianity, goods were held in common; there was a detachment from ownership. Stewardship was the operative word. The needs both of the small communities as well as those found in the larger villages, towns and cities had to be addressed if the early Christians were to be faithful to Christ's example of feeding, healing and comforting.

Over the past one hundred years, a vast body of Catholic social teachings has brought that attitude sharply into focus. It is not that Successful Catholics can quote from the many social encyclicals and letters, but the underlying messages of these documents permeate their lives. They are willing to take the risks that discipleship entails. They give of themselves when it is not always convenient or comfortable, even when it might entail risk. Successful Catholics are willing to look at the larger issue of societal ills and attempt to redress the imbalance between those who have and those who have not, whether the needs be material, emotional or spiritual.

Today, we within the Christian commonwealth live differently from our counterparts in the days of the apostles, but that sense of detachment from what happens to be in our hands for this hour, day or year is still embedded in Catholic life. Survival of the fittest might explain the evolution of the animal kingdom, but it is not how the kingdom of God was designed to function.

God created us for each other, to help each other, to inspire each other. That help and inspiration are forthcoming in the many small acts that are sprinkled through Successful Catholics' days. Many times almost imperceptible, these acts create an atmosphere that there are in our midst human beings who care enough about other human beings—family and stranger alike—to set their own needs aside and look to the needs, spoken or silent, of others.

For John Mazurski, an opportunity came one afternoon when he was washing up after the workday. A fellow worker was trying to wash up, but he had a huge bandage on one hand. No one was helping him. Mazurski walked over, took the man's dirty hand, soaped it, rinsed it off and walked away.

Real Life, Spiritual Life

Those good—and terribly misunderstood—nuns who taught so many of today's Successful Catholics have gotten decidedly mixed reviews. They may not have known the subtleties of human growth and development, but they knew well that human beings have a remarkable range. And only when people are stretched, asked to give beyond what they think they can afford physically and emotionally will they grow into fully functioning, empathetic, kind, good people. If allowed to believe their own limitations, their souls shrink and atrophy. If encouraged and sometimes nudged to soar, they sprout amazing wings.

Successful Catholics see this clearly. They see the reason for being called out of themselves, for being continually beckoned to transcend their limitations.

After listening to the life stories of those whom I now call Successful Catholics, I can attest to their realization that while rich and fruitful religious and spiritual lives might be centered in a faith community or parish, very little of their lives are actually spent there. Very few opportunities are presented to change the world in those places. Rather, it is at town meetings, while reading a newspaper or overhearing conversations that they are given the option to do something—or not. It is in these moments that Successful Catholics show the depth of their beliefs. Holiness is dailiness.

A Catholic woman lawyer who supervises an office full of men—men who are unhappy to have not only a Hispanic boss, but a woman boss as well—realizes what she must do. She talks of not just getting the job done, but "loving" her reluctant coworkers in the process, even though they would prefer she weren't there at all. It is extraordinarily difficult, but she sees it as exactly what she has to do if her faith means anything to her at all. This is where the spiritual tire hits the road of life for her.

Thomas Huntley is my fellow parishioner and a retired executive. I knew that he helped out as an usher in church, but one day when I talked about this "secret"—Successful Catholics being called out of themselves—I found that he was involved in many other volunteer activities, one of which was his faithful visits to nursing home patients. He had seen too many retirees dedicate themselves to golf or socializing, because they felt that this was their reward for many years of work, and thought that a life of leisure would bring them happiness. "It just didn't work for me," he said. "I have to do things for others so the selfish me doesn't take over. And when I do things for others, I'm really getting so much out of it myself."

The image of water flowing into a lake comes to mind. Only if that water—think of it as the blessings and graces we all receive—eventually has a place to go will the lake itself remain fresh. We actually *need* to let those blessings and graces flow through us.

It may be the dailiness of dealing with a difficult child or an aging parent, it may be in the work place, where Catholic morals and decency may appear at times to be irrelevant to the task at hand. Wherever it is, Successful Catholics see these as opportunities, difficult as they may be, to put into practice a way of life so ingrained within them.

Vanessa Cooke, a counselor in a prestigious high school, spends some of her spare hours working with children of poverty whose parents are drug addicts and prostitutes. Leon Roberts brought a group of alienated college students back to the church through his work with a choir. Dorothy Papachristos befriended the very gang members who burned down her restaurant. There is an amazing diversity in what Successful Catholics do. Yet there is a similarity. Their activities are a natural outgrowth of a faith that cries out to be expressed in everyday life. "How else can I show God I care?" asks Vanessa.

Statistics and Reality

As surveys tell their sad story of Americans giving less of their time and their money to charity, it is little wonder that some see as the outcome for such selfishness a broad-based national malaise, with resulting self-doubt about our inherent goodness. But it is the Successful Catholic who continues to do his or her quiet, unassuming, yet powerful part—a crucial component of their own personal and mysterious spiritual blend. I have not found Successful Catholics to be righteous about their actions or partisan about their ends. For the most part, they are not people with an agenda, as if their good deeds were guaranteed to produce the changes that they hope for in their secular or church world.

I rarely have heard such words as "evangelization" or "vocations" on their lips. They are not looking for converts; they are constantly converting themselves. They simply do what they do. Meanwhile, there is a quiet, yet readily apparent religious authority about Successful Catholics that goes to the very core of humanity, bringing hope and holiness, light and lightness into daily life. The effects of these many words, acts and thoughts we may never really know or understand. But these Successful Catholics—and those they have touched—experience a glow that clearly radiates the presence of God in our midst.

Further Thought and Action

Reflection

We have learned that a life spent caring only about ourselves is a small and ultimately joyless life. When we reach out to other people, lend a hand, provide something they cannot provide for themselves—be it something material or something psychological or spiritual—we, too, are enriched. It is so true that in giving we receive. As we need help from others, others need help from us. And, there is a marvelous quality about giving for others—giving begets giving. It spreads, and encourages other people to tap their own pools of generosity and goodness. What a warm glow we feel when we put our needs aside and tend to the needs of someone else.

Just Imagine...

...you are one of those people traveling on the road written about in scripture so many years ago who sees someone lying in a ditch, beaten by robbers. No one is around. No one will ever know if you simply pass by. After all, this is a person that you or your people have nothing to do with and, in fact, hate. But, looking at that person lying there, suddenly instead of his or her face, you see your own, bruised and bloody. For an instant, the roles are reversed. Just as quickly it is over, but you cannot forget that momentary transposition. What would you want someone to do for you if you were lying beside the road? What does your heart tell you to do?

Words to Ponder:

"As you did it to one of the least of these my brethren, you did it to me."

Questions to Ponder:

✚ Why does Jesus ask us to be concerned about other people? Isn't my life difficult enough without having to look out for others?

✚ Can I remember a time that someone really put themselves out to help me? What was my reaction?

✚ When did I "go the extra mile" for someone else? In giving, did I receive?

A Prayer

"Dear Lord, there are two people within me. One is selfish, the other is not. In the depths of my heart I want to be a giving person, ready to help other people, because, quite honestly, I know how much I need that kindness from others. If goodness doesn't begin with me, it doesn't begin at all. Help me to reach ever deeper into my own resources—for you have given me so much in life—so that I can share what I have with the men and women who cross my path.

Help me to see you in others, for when I look into their eyes, I look into your own."

If Not Yet Yours,
Making This Secret Your Own

The next twenty-four hours will offer the opportunity to be called out of yourself. Usually it will be nothing large or heroic, but it can be a beginning. It may be something as simple as saying nothing when someone criticizes a coworker; or you might even offer something positive about that person. You may see a neighborhood child doing something that parents should know about. There may be a coworker who is obviously having a hard time, and you may be in a position to ease his or her way. Or you may find yourself called upon for something more, such as confronting an injustice you see that you simply know is wrong.

If It Already Is,
A Way to Deepen the Secret

You already know how necessary it is for you to be called out of yourself for other people. Now it is time to make such an action, your next one, truly loving. Do it not out of a sense of obligation, but out of love for another. View him in an entirely different light; see her as a total, complex human being, just as you would hope to be viewed. Perform whatever task it is, but do it with a renewed sense of real affection for that person. After all, that person is the means not only to your salvation, but your happiness as well.

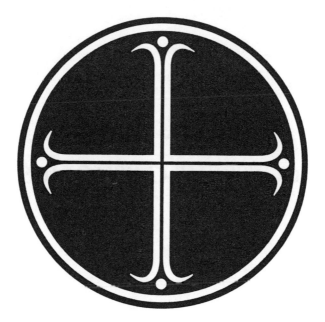

5

SUCCESSFUL CATHOLICS...

Always remember that God is ultimately merciful and forgiving.

Yes, Successful Catholics feel God's finger in their backs, urging them on to perfection. The example of Christ, the church's social teachings, thoughtful homilies and the lives of the saints all testify that Catholicism is continually demanding one's best; it is not a leisure-time activity. But as strongly as Successful Catholics feel God's not-always-so-gentle urgings, they feel his mercy and pardon even more. The God they know is not some sort of fire-breathing judge or divine bookkeeper who keeps strict tally of their failures, but rather a God whose mercy is embarrassingly deep and readily available.

Successful Catholics are no strangers to self-reflection: they recognize all too well their shortcomings, sometimes even in the very areas I've just been laying out as their secret strengths. But they have the confidence that no matter how miserably they behave, they can never, ever exile themselves beyond the reach of the love and forgiveness of God.

"You should never leave the church because you're in a state of sin," says Gail Smith, a grade-school teacher and mother. "That's absolutely the wrong way to look at it and one of the most misunderstood things in the church. The church is exactly the right place for sinners. We're all sinners and that's why we need to be together."

Before Their God

"O, Lord I am not worthy to receive you, but only say the word and I shall be healed." Successful Catholics humbly acknowledge the first part of those well-known words spoken before the eucharist is received—and boldly claim the second. They know they are guilty of many and varied acts of omission or commission, and while they might feel pretty miserable about their failings, they have learned that to wallow in guilt is both counterproductive and an outright rejection of God's embrace. After all, they *know* they will be healed, forgiven and accepted. And how else could it be? If God is indeed a loving father, would he do less than a worldly father? Would he continue to hold children to whom he gave life at some unreachable distance, especially when they cry out that they need him so desperately?

Successful Catholics all across this land do not think so. And they are not shy about calling out to God, confident of forgiveness, ready to start afresh. They ask and it is theirs. God, to them, has a short, a *very* short memory of their failings. God is encouraging about their future, not bent on dragging them through the past. Those Successful Catholics who are parents (and all, of course, were once children themselves) need only think of a child approaching a parent and saying, "I'm sorry. I did wrong. I want to do better," for their hearts to burst open with forgiveness and love. It is that kind of tender, understanding relationship that they feel with a forgiving and loving God.

"There's nothing we can do that alienates us from God," says Bob Dwyer, a lawyer. "Through wrongdoing we might alienate ourselves from ourselves and from other people, but God is always there for us. When we sin it makes us unhappy. That is what we feel. God hasn't gone anywhere. He's standing by, waiting, ready to forgive and embrace us."

For Dorothea Tobin, the mother of seven, not allowing God to forgive her is actually an act of selfishness. "It happens when I convince myself I don't need to turn to God for grace, that I can get myself out of this mess. But when I get by my selfishness, it's like a cool breeze washing over me."

I treasure the story of Father James Healy as a living example of exactly what the presence of God can mean in our darkest hour. When he was a boy, his father had failed to show up for an altar server assignment because his own father needed him at home that particular morning. The pastor would hear of no such excuse and commanded the boy to kneel at the altar rail throughout an entire Sunday mass for his penance. The boy was humiliated; he wished he were dead. But kneeling there in full public view, he felt a hand on his shoulder. He looked over. There was his father kneeling beside him.

That is how Successful Catholics visualize God. He is always with them, in their best moments and their worst, when they are virtuous and when they are sinners, when the world applauds them, and when they are scorned.

It seems to me that Successful Catholics have been able to work through natural doubts about their abilities to develop a mature faith in a higher power than their own. They understand that God did not create his people perennially to linger one virtuous act away from acceptance. They do not look at the relationship with God as "so much legalism," as college professor Dick Westly puts it. "We have to be careful not to lose the concept of sin because it is very important that we realize we can rupture the relationship with

God and with each other through our actions. But, as for being unable to repair that relationship: impossible."

For many Successful Catholics, the new understanding of the sacrament of reconciliation provides a way to bring their sins before God and into the midst of their community. For sin is not only individual, but communal as well, and Successful Catholics, being a sacramental people, know that herein lies an opportunity to lay down their burdens and be infused with grace.

"I think the mercy of God is his greatest attribute," says Lena Shipley. How great and unfathomable it must be. How sad when we fail to trust it. Just think of St. Peter and Judas. Both betrayed Christ. One trusted in his mercy and became the first pope of the Roman Catholic Church. The other hung himself."

Before Themselves

What also helps Successful Catholics in this relationship with an ultimately forgiving and loving God is having a sense of detachment, charity—and humor—both about themselves and their church. How can individuals obsess upon personal failures when they sense a God who loves them desperately and will never turn from them? Successful Catholics have the ability to stand outside their lives and look with affection upon themselves as struggling individuals. "My goodness, he did that?" "She what? Really!" Successful Catholics are able to laugh at their frequent, unvirtuous fits and starts. And they can quietly marvel at their occasional transcendence.

"The most unkind and unmerciful person in our lives will always be ourself," says Matt Doyle. "But I never have believed most people are actually capable of committing grievous sins. When we are able to let ourselves off the hook, then we get the picture of what God must truly be like."

Always remember that God is ultimately merciful and forgiving.

Successful Catholics are people who are—and this might be a strange way to put it—*optimistic* about sin. They realize that once sin is acknowledged, an apology to God is already half rendered. The relationship is already on the mend. They are not people who feel that God will love them more if they continually stir up their misdeeds in a warmed-over stew of self-incrimination. As Thomas Merton, Trappist monk, writer and first-class sinner expressed the concept of God that eventually saved him: "Mercy within mercy within mercy."

The failures of this life—and Successful Catholics are not shy about detailing their own lengthy lists—are not the measure of who they are as people. It is their *desire* to be better people, not their *success* at achieving this end. As sometimes futile as their efforts might be, and disastrous the results, Successful Catholics are still believers in their perfectibility.

Successful Catholics are not people who require a lot of praise for who they are and what they do, nor are they hobbled by their mistakes. What I have found is a quiet confidence with their "habit of being." It is not smug, not satisfied, but always searching, always seeking, ready to get on with the great and small opportunities that present themselves each day. They have a sense of worth in their own eyes. They humbly believe that God also sees their worth.

Before Their Church

Because their understanding of God's mercy informs an acceptance of themselves, Successful Catholics can also look with equal charity upon their church. This magnificent body of believers, this pilgrim people, has had quite a venerable but sometimes checkered history. The church is made up of the morally upright and the weak. Yes, it is divinely inspired and divinely anointed, but so achingly human, with too many faulty decisions on its ledgers. Yet, the Catholic Church has, perhaps more than any institution on the face of the earth, stood on the side of the poor and downtrodden, spoken up for those with no voice and been the most vocal and visible advocate for morality ever seen in history. And Successful Catholics are a proud part of that universal church.

The Successful Catholic both reveres the church in all its majesty and forgives it for its shortcomings. And it is this combination of idealism and reality—of faithfulness combined with thoughtfulness—that allows Successful Catholics to be part of a church that calls out to them, not with a single voice but with many voices, sometimes confusing and sometimes even contradictory. No longer is this the Catholic Church that older Successful Catholics remember from their youth, a Catholic Church with precise answers to all questions.

But, I have found, amidst all the differing opinions, the threats of damnation and the promises of reward, that Successful Catholics are people who are able to still the cacophony and set aside the rhetorical clutter, holding on to the essence of what Catholic belief is all about. They are able to fathom what the life of Jesus Christ really means. Successful Catholics are those who can see that the words and example of Jesus in scripture are more a message of healing and forgiveness than a threat of punishment. As they sit in their pews at mass or read the ancient words in the quiet of their homes, they are continually impressed and refreshed by a God who demands so much, yet accepts them in all their frailty. Each of them is the lost sheep, sought until found—the prodigal embraced.

They know that Jesus concentrated his wrath not on struggling sinners, but on the hypocrites—those supposedly holy ones whose actions appeared so righteous, yet whose inner dispositions were so flawed. Sinners they may be, but the Successful Catholics I've met are certainly not hypocrites.

Always remember that God is ultimately merciful and forgiving.

It is not that Successful Catholics look upon God as some sort of cosmic patsy who blithely accepts anything they do. They are aware of their own hollow attempts to extract from him a "cheap forgiveness." They shudder at the thought of God's displeasure, but what motivates them is something far more fertile, alive, positive, energizing. They know that while fear of God might discipline their actions, it is the love of God—and the sense of God's love for them—that will truly inspire and motivate them in their lives. They fear not so much the darkness as they seek the light.

Further Thought and Action

Reflection

Throughout the New Testament, time and time again, Jesus speaks of mercy and forgiveness. Those the world looked upon as sinners were among his closest friends. Only the hypocrites—those who displayed no need for forgiveness, because they thought they were already perfect—did he consistently condemn. As Jesus is the human personification of God, he represents God's nature. So it is clear that God, while demanding moral excellence, is ultimately forgiving. A loving father, he knows the human nature of his children all too well. And, as a father, he wants to forgive so that his children can go on, unburdened by the memories of their failures, heartened instead by his concern for them.

Just Imagine...

...you are walking alongside Jesus as he encounters people in his travels—prostitutes, tax collectors, lepers, common fishermen. These are hardly the cream of society. He talks to each of them so kindly, so gently, as if they were royalty. He sees something in each of them, something the human eye does not easily reveal. Although he himself is a holy man, he does not accuse them of wrongdoing, of not living as he does. He just seems happy to see them. And this seems to release them from their faults and shortcomings. They, too, are happy to see him. What are they saying to him? And what does he say in return?

Words to Ponder:

"I ask for mercy not sacrifice, a loving heart rather than holocausts."

Questions to Ponder:

✚ How can it be that God is so forgiving? Does this mean that there really are no standards, that I can do anything and if I ask for forgiveness, it is mine?
✚ When have I felt most outside God's mercy?
✚ When have I experienced God's "mercy within mercy within mercy"?

A Prayer

"Dear Lord, your mercy toward me is nothing short of embarrassing. I have sinned so many times and committed the same sins over and over. And I will probably commit them again. Yet, your words and your example keep reminding me that there is nothing I do that can ever put me outside your love. I know that you forgive me. Help me to forgive myself for the things I do. And let me come to you quickly in the future whenever I fall. I know your hand is there to help me up."

If Not Yet Yours,
Making This Secret Your Own

Think of the worst thing you have ever done, something for which you even have trouble forgiving yourself. Would you not forgive a person of this if they sincerely said, "I'm sorry." Say that "I'm sorry" to God. Be quiet. Let the mercy of God wash over you.

If It Already Is,
A Way to Deepen the Secret

You already know of God's mercy for you. You have felt this healing presence. What a source of comfort it has been in your life. Now you are able to extend the mercy you have felt. Is there someone in your life from whom you have withheld forgiveness for something done to you, or to someone you love? Is this the time to be the conduit through which God's mercy is transmitted? As you have been forgiven, can you forgive?

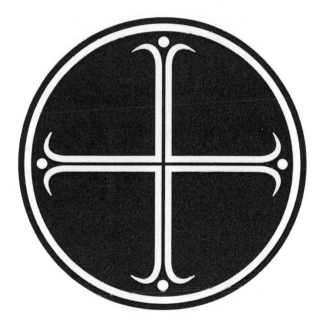

6
SUCCESSFUL CATHOLICS...

Live in the moment, recognizing daily opportunities for holiness.

In these dizzying times, Catholics are alternately tempted to retreat to the comforting shelter of the Old Church—(to have such surety in unsure times!)—or to plunge blindly forward onto the exhilarating open meadows of the New Church—(what promise, what possibilities!). Church reform isn't coming quickly enough, a group of Catholics say in one breath; but this, this has gone too far, another group says with the next. Cautionary calls for church discipline mingle with a primal scream for freedom and trust.

Successful Catholics live in this conflict between a past time—when life seemed brighter, simpler and easier—and a much cloudier future. But recalling what was and looking ahead to what might be, they know that neither really exists. Yes, memories inform their judgements and hope drives them on, but there is only today as the blank slate to be written upon. The Successful Catholic is determined that, with all the imponderables and difficulties that today presents, and as imperfectly as human knowledge and judgements may be, this day and this day alone provides a slate to be written upon.

What they can shape are themselves, their family, their workplace, their faith community—the small but crucial part of the world that they inhabit. Successful Catholics are pragmatic, believers in

71

the vision that they are cocreators with God of this world. But they are also pragmatic dreamers, constantly attempting to find better ways to act, to be holier people. They take seriously the mandate that none of us is an island; our actions are ripples that reach far beyond where we might imagine.

Most Successful Catholics do not imagine themselves some latter-day Damien of Molokai, who worked with the lepers, or St. Martin de Porres, who ministered to slaves, or modern-day saints such as Mother Teresa or Dorothy Day. They are not hermits or martyrs or monks. Their aims might seem smaller, more immediate, more commonplace, but are they less admirable? I think not. Successful Catholics are not people who wait for the perfect time, the perfect circumstance to exercise their goodness. To them, gospel values are timeless and clear, and opportunities to live them out are presented throughout each day. While life is a mysterious adventure to us all, the Successful Catholic chooses to embrace that mystery fully, to look for holiness in the seemingly commonplace, in the people, events and circumstances of life.

A lay group of Successful Catholics at the National Center for the Laity puts it this way:

> "There is a unique treasure imprinted in the imagination of every Catholic. It is the suspicion that embedded in the ordinary lies the extraordinary, the miraculous, the salvific....Catholics see the shopping mall, the schoolhouse, the kitchen table, the factory, the courtroom and the hospital as altars of sorts—places where the ordinary mundane labors of life may be offered up, blessed and transformed into things of beauty....God is related to each of us...many times a day, thousands of times in a lifetime, in every ordinary encounter."

Successful Catholics look back to the life of Christ and see that his miracles were performed in the most ordinary of circumstances—at a wedding feast, on the road, on a boat ride. He encountered common people in the commonplace situations of their lives. Successful Catholics may not be able to cure physical blindness or raise the dead or multiply loaves and fishes, but their actions have their own miraculous power when gospel values come alive in their own lives.

Holy Places All

On her postal route Rose Mary Hart takes a little extra time for the elderly shut-ins. She realizes she may be the only person they will see today. While Maxine Dennis, a cashier in a supermarket, totals and bags groceries, she always pays attention to the looks on her customers' faces and the tone of their voices. She is a competent worker, but it is compassion that she sees as the most important tool she brings to work each day. Joseph Sciortino, the CEO of a computer systems company, tries to look at each of the many workers in his huge business as an individual, with individual talents—and needs.

Delivering the mail could be measured by the severity of the weather or the number of bulk mail pieces; the checkout counter could be a matter of putting in the required hours with a minimum of emotional gratification; and running a computer company could be driven by the need to succeed and survive in a highly competitive field. But Successful Catholics such as these, and many more like them across the country, simply do not see their work merely as an economic necessity. Yes, they must do their very best, but they see beyond mere performance or accomplishment. They see in their work life a place to put their Catholic beliefs into practice. They see human interactions as occasions for grace, both for themselves and those with whom they are dealing.

The theologian Karl Rahner used the term "everyday mysticism" to describe how God was surprisingly present all around us; only our failure to sense his presence prevented these connections from being made. For what is mysticism but an encounter with the divine, both in wondrous events, moments and people as well as in the tragedies and sorrows that are part of our lives. Through a certain intentionality and constant reflection, encounters with God can occur all the time.

Successful Catholics have found that the worlds of work, family and religious expression are not segmented, with each requiring a different moral outlook. They are part of the seamless cloth of life, holy places all, communities of God's creatures. Each world has an effect on the others. The parish council president who is a terrible boss or the regular churchgoer who makes inferior products sends out clear messages about the lack of depth of their beliefs.

And for CEO Sciortino, it goes even further, for here is a man whose actions are constantly being watched. He knows he is a role model and his example will form the people around him. The organization mirrors his image and so his "business vocation" is to be honest, ethical and moral. Marty Geraghty, a commercial real estate agent, echoes this sentiment. "Honesty is a great challenge in my business; there is the constant temptation to gloss over things. I must be honest if my faith means anything at all. What kind of father am I to my children if I do things myself that I ask them not to do? You can't leave honesty home at the doorstep and then expect to pick it up when you return."

It is this interrelatedness that Successful Catholics attempt to achieve. They realize that they spend more time at work than any other place in their lives, more than with their family, far more than the time in church or at prayer.

Bill Droel, who has been active in the National Center for the Laity's efforts to help people see the connection between their faith lives and their work lives, says, "It's not so much about quote bringing Christ to the workplace unquote. Rather it's a case of discovering the grace that is already there. Catholics just need to exercise their sacramental imagination to uncover God in everyday events. That meeting where people are tearing each other apart—well, maybe all the tensions have to get out, but that doesn't prevent you from saying something comforting to that somebody who got pretty beaten up in the process. It's that simple and that profound."

Specific. Individual. Successful Catholics find few occasions in their lives for grand, redeeming, heroic acts. Matt Doyle reflects on a lesson he learned when he worked in radio: he tries never to forget who is on the other side of the microphone. "When I see no one or 'all of you' out there, I lose the proper perspective," he says. "I must talk to one person, deal with one person at a time."

At Home

In this age when the popular culture can be such a dominant voice in children's lives, Successful Catholics are all the more aware of how important it is to make their homes havens from a mindless secularism and to transform ordinary family interactions into occasions for a natural, organic kind of religious instruction. At the home of David and Nancy Foley, dinner table talk about current events—and how Catholic values can be applied—is encouraged. Even talk of how the church is failing to meet people's needs is welcomed, as are differing views on such touchy issues as birth control and divorce. For the Foleys, this is exactly the moment that one generation can speak to the other about how life is going along each of their roads.

Joan Sullivan's foster children were predominantly non-Catholic, so since they could not receive the eucharist, she made it a practice upon returning from the altar to touch them on the head. One

Sunday, one of her teenagers was extremely hostile and angry and she didn't touch him after the eucharist. He looked up sadly and said, "You're not going to touch me?" That simple touch, with the eucharist so fresh within her, had a power she had not realized.

Successful Catholics see the power in signs and rituals. They observe or create rituals in their homes—from Advent calendars to inviting each member of the gathering to pray at special times. Ethnic traditions are seeing a wonderful resurgence. Successful Catholics often display religious art—whether Michelangelo or Dali, a treasured heirloom crucifix or a modern cross—in their homes to remind them of who they are and where their power and inspiration come from. Some have tasteful religious art or posters in their offices. When Malc Sills retired, he gave his coworkers holy cards with the prayer of St. Francis of Assisi. Many gave them prominent places at their work stations. They remember him and his parting gift to this day.

Joan Sullivan's touch, Malc Sills's holy cards and Maxine Dennis's compassionate concern are just some examples of the many ways that Successful Catholics recognize the opportunities to impart holiness in everyday life. For other Successful Catholics, it was what some might consider a tragedy that transformed them. They did not have the luxury of choosing to live in the moment. They were given a far greater—and continuing—challenge.

When Peter Hebein was told that the child he and his wife had so long awaited had Down's Syndrome, he looked inward and saw an impatient, demanding man—one who found it difficult to accept anything less than perfection. "But Chris was put in our lives for a very special reason," he says. "I'm not the same person today. I changed. I see people in a way I never did before. You can't live with a Down's child day in and day out and not see God's hand at work."

Live in the moment, recognizing daily opportunities for holiness.

Further Thought and Action

Reflection

Ours is life lived in the present tense. Memories may be precious or painful, intentions lofty or low, but all we really have to live is today. Each day, each hour brings with it opportunities for our spirits to soar, for us to become the people we know we can be. So much of life may seem commonplace, routine, ordinary. We may not seem to have opportunities for real greatness or heroism. But, of course, we do. Daily, hourly. With our desire and good will and imagination, we have the potential to transform, to make holy everything we touch, every person we meet.

Just Imagine...

...you have been traveling with Jesus and his friends. One afternoon a huge crowd of some five thousand people gathers and Jesus begins to speak to them of the ways of his father. He speaks for hours; the people are taken with his power, authority and genuineness. But now his talk is over. As they were hungry for his words, they are now hungry for food. The apostles are impatient with the crowd; how are they supposed to feed so many? Jesus takes five barley loaves and two dried fish. He blesses them. His hand reaches out to pass the food. What do you see happening?

Words to Ponder:

"If there is any path at all on which I can approach You, it must lead through the very middle of my ordinary daily life. If You have given me no single place to which I can flee and be sure of finding You, then I must be able to find You in every place in each and every thing I do."–Karl Rahner
Prayers for a Lifetime (New York: Crossroad, 1984), 91.

Questions to Ponder

✛ It's so tiring to have to make the most out of every situation. Wouldn't it be better if I just concentrated on those around me–my family and my friends?
✛ After all, I'm just one person. What effect can I really have?
✛ When have I seen the presence of God in an unexpected place?

A Prayer

"Dear Lord, your grace, your presence are all around me. It is only my lack of vision and faith that prevents me from seeing you in the everyday occurrences of my life. Open my eyes. Open my heart. Let me not only see you working in the world, but to be about that work myself. After all, I am made in your image; I was made to be holy and to make this world holy. Help me to work miracles in the ordinariness of my life."

Live in the moment, recognizing daily opportunities for holiness.

If It Is Not Yet Yours,
Making This Secret Your Own

Sometimes it is hard to see that you can bring holiness into the world. But today, as you go to work, come home or wherever you may be, you will see an opportunity. It may present itself in an instant, asking your response or action right then. Holiness is already there; but suddenly you will see it. You will know you have been given this opportunity to experience God's presence or to bring his peace or healing or kindness to someone else. Do your best to see the holiness of that moment.

If It Already Is,
A Way to Deepen the Secret

When you begin to see holiness in everyday life, it is as if a new light was shed on things that you couldn't see before. But there is more light yet to be shed, and more opportunities to make the world a holy place. Look in places you may not have considered before for these opportunities. Let the Spirit guide you in the days ahead. There are areas of your life yet to be sanctified. There are places where God's presence is so hungrily sought—and you can be the vehicle for that. Look back on the day and see where the moments of holiness occurred. Did you see them then? What might you have done differently?

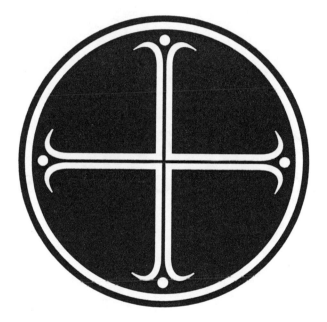

7

SUCCESSFUL CATHOLICS...

Believe in prayer and pray regularly.

Perhaps this, the last secret of Successful Catholics, is the most important secret of all. For what is prayer but a continuing communication with God. It is water to pierce the dryness of souls, nutrients that allow the human spirit to strengthen and flower; it is encouragement to go on.

The prayer lives of Successful Catholics are anything but ordinary or standardized. Rather, their prayer lives represent a rich smorgasbord of spirituality. But whatever their method or approach might be, Successful Catholics consider prayer absolutely crucial to their moral well-being. In the end, it is prayer—this continuing divine connection—that allows Successful Catholics to flourish.

It may be the corporate executive who rises a half hour earlier than her family to meditate before her work day sweeps her away, or the man with a rosary playing through his fingers before mass. It may be those carefully studying the Bible on the subway, verse by verse; or those meditating in the lotus position, eyes closed. Written prayers, silent prayers, devotional prayers, the prayer of simple silence and presence before the Lord, reflection, contemplation, a thoughtful examination of the day's events and a considered response to them. A prayer at bedside or at the family dinner table, in the car or elevator, while nursing an infant or taking a walk. A prayer, with candles burning, before a statue of the Virgin or a favorite saint. Prayer has many forms.

To the Successful Catholic, prayer is so necessary that its lack creates an almost chemical imbalance. It is so difficult to make decisions, distinguish the important from the trival, savor life's triumphs or weather its failures with the equanimity that all Catholics hope to achieve. It is hard, Successful Catholics readily admit, to be able to perform those actions that call them outside of themselves and to avoid walking down those enticing roads that lead to predictable dead ends. Prayer makes the crucial difference in their lives.

The Great Change, the Great Connection

In a Catholicism that many still remember, the object of prayers (not really *praying*) was to pile up some imaginary storehouse of spiritual treasures in heaven, so that we wretched human beings, against all odds, might eke out our eternal reward. Prayer was routinized, institutionalized and some would even say trivialized by the emphasis on form rather than content, an exercise in precision, rather than an attempt to link the human heart to the heart of God. Father Thomas Keating, the Trappist monk and author who has shaped the spirituality of many Successful Catholics, said in an interview that there was enormous dissatisfaction "...with ordinary religion...which is more moralistic than really nourishing of the spiritual needs of many people."

Gradually, Successful Catholics have replaced the concept of the penurious, unpleasable, bookkeeper God with a personal God who offers them an open account that they can draw on at any time. Their channel is prayer, being in the presence of God, talking to God, listening to God. It is this approach to prayer that has refreshed and continues to refresh the spiritual and secular lives of Successful Catholics.

Younger Catholics readily come to this sense of God's openness and availability. Many are not products of Catholic education, but they are becoming aware of the vast treasure-house of spirituality their church possesses. And younger Successful Catholics are finding paths of prayer that resonate within their deepest being, allowing them to touch the God who first calls out to them.

Although the word "mysticism" was once seen as an exclusive approach to God open only to the sainted, Successful Catholics–both young and old–have found it to be a path that they too can follow. For what is mysticism but a connection with God? Successful Catholics *are* mystics, mystics who work at jobs, go to school, raise families, shop at the supermarket, read the newspaper, get tired, lose their patience. And it is prayer that allows them to sense that God is not some inaccessible presence beyond the narrowest of gates (although that biblical phrase is one that they understand as constantly demanding their best effort), but rather readily available anytime they want, standing before them, awaiting them with open arms.

Many Catholics once hesitated at beginning a prayer life, feeling they would not choose the right words or would pray for the wrong things. Successful Catholics were among them; but they found if they waited for the perfect moment or the perfect words, the prayers that were burning in their hearts would never be offered. Instead, with perhaps no more than a deep groaning in their souls or by uttering the word "Help!", they were willing to reach out their hands to God's hand.

Prayer, for the Successful Catholic, is seldom a magnificent paean to the divine. Prayer can be a plea, a conversation, an acknowledgement of the Almighty or simply a way of saying thanks. It can also involve a lot of daydreaming and periods of extraordinary dryness. As Successful Catholics are no strangers to their imperfections, they have learned to live with an imperfect, sometimes truncated prayer life. They try to pray regularly and sometimes they are successful. Many times they have to admit they are not. But they pray, knowing that God's mercy and attention are theirs.

Different Seasons

God is one, but with many names. And, likewise, there are many moods and seasons of Successful Catholics' prayer lives. Sometimes they can almost touch God and are filled with a bliss beyond telling. At other times, God is distant, and their words are hollow and dry. The prayer of the factory worker and the prayer of the corporate executive may be different, but Successful Catholics do not struggle for uniformity, do not strive to "do it right." God calls each of us by our own name. Successful Catholics, with their own unique needs, eventually develop a confidence to speak in their own voices.

"At the age of twenty-three I prayed for a husband in that old 'magic' way," says Mary Anne Barry, who is now a grandmother. "Then over the years that faded and I began to be so aware of the presence of God in the natural things of my life—my children, plants, sunlight. I could pray about almost anything, anytime. But when my husband became sick, it all seemed to leave me; I just dried up spiritually. Thankfully, I belong to a prayer group and they prayed when I couldn't, and that was what brought me through those days. Prayer is so mysterious. And so necessary."

The Successful Catholic knows that by seeking God in prayer, he or she has already made the connection. God is always there first, waiting. God asks no more than an open heart; and that is what prayer is—an opening of our being to that Being, however and whenever it occurs.

Believe in prayer and pray regularly.

An Attitude, Not an Action

Prayer, for Successful Catholics, is rarely some intense, transcendent experience. Much of the time, prayers that target a specific goal are not answered. "To me, prayer is always having God in my heart," says Numa Torres, whose daughter contracted meningitis at the age of two and was made deaf. "God may not restore her hearing, but he will always help me, regardless of what happens. That is more important than getting this or that which I ask for. God knows better than I. He takes care of you."

So it is not so much prayer as *prayerfulness* that is the bedrock of Successful Catholics' spirituality; it is an attitude, not just an action. "Pray always" was an admonition that many Catholics heard in their religious training, but Successful Catholics have found that this does not necessarily mean a constant march of rosary beads through anxious fingers or the omniscient mumbling of prayers beneath one's breath. Rather, it is that attempt to be at once in contact with God as with their deepest selves, to pray in church and before meetings, to pray before a tough decision or in a traffic jam, to constantly make that connection, oftentimes wordlessly or even without a specific thought or request.

Successful Catholics have been brought to a "life of prayer" through many life experiences—from parenthood to aging, alcoholism to divorce, a gnawing spiritual hunger or a serendipitous moment of sensing the presence of God; but once the need has been acknowledged and the connection (or the attempts at the connection) made, their lives are changed. "Religion is for people who are afraid of going to hell," says Darrell Colbert, speaking of his spiritual path; "prayer is for those who have already been to hell." A confessed substance abuser of the first rank, when Colbert attempted suicide—and awoke to find he hadn't succeeded—his first thoughts raced back to his childhood. When times were bad, he used to hide

87

in a small loft behind the altar of his local parish church and talk to God. He went back to that loft in his mind, and prayed. He is now a counselor and says prayers to St. Jude and St. Francis every day. "God can't fail," he says; "my life is proof of that."

Prayer for Successful Catholics is a mystical coat of many colors. For some, like Colbert, it is rooted in devotions to the saints who saved him. Others say the breviary, attend mass, meditate, listen more than they speak. Dee Harris, who sells cars, has a well-worn Bible on his desk, next to his interest rate book. "Not that I'm one of these religious fanatics," he says; "I just need to pick it up during the day when things are going bad. Something always speaks to me."

Many Successful Catholics take special times away to pray; some go to monasteries; others to the ocean shore. Some pray alone; others are faithful members of Bible study or prayer groups, some in existence as long as twenty-five years. As different as all of these communications with God might be, what underlies the prayer lives of these Successful Catholics is that while saying formal prayers or personal prayers, or just listening, their hearts are inclined to God. It is this deep sentiment of their hearts that will never be denied.

Rich Fruits of Prayerfulness

Joan Sullivan has worked in drug rehabilitation, raised foster children and faced the sometimes painful loneliness of a single woman. "But if I take a moment to pray or meditate or just to be conscious of what is going on around me, somehow something bigger than me comes through and I can do things I just didn't think were possible."

It is that quiet but sure sense of power—not necessarily success or blessings or the gaining of things asked for—that Successful

Catholics, in many different ways, describe as the rich and continuing harvest of a prayer life.

Shilpi D'Costa says the same prayer before going out onto the streets of Washington, D.C. that she did as a child walking the dusty roads of rural Bangladesh. "Lord be with me when I walk." That prayer has bridged thousands of miles and enfolded her within two very different cultures. It is not the place or circumstances that really alter the sense of connection to God for these Successful Catholics.

But, as a good number of them would attest, prayerfulness does not always produce serenity, peace or surety. "Sometimes when I pray to God for guidance in my life I see the big picture," says Vanessa Cooke. "That's the scariest gift of all—when I see what I have to do about it."

For Marty Hegarty, it is when he *stops* praying that praying begins to work. "Only then does it take flesh as I go out into the world," he says. "I have no objectives, really, nor do I lay out impossible goals. If there is something I can do or say that will make life better for you, then I'm living up to the grace in me. I guess that's the way I live out my prayer life."

The prayer lives of Successful Catholics are not guided by some form of spiritual management-by-objective approach or the "name it and claim it" school of praying. It is not *what* Successful Catholics receive from prayerfulness, but *how* they are because they pray. God is not changed by our prayers; we are. It is that "habit of being" that we talked about at the beginning. "By their fruits you shall know them" is a true barometer for Successful Catholics, a true indicator of the potency of their prayer lives. Prayerfulness brings a peace of mind, both a genuineness and a depth to relationships, a certain intelligent humility, an excitement to life and a trust—both in one's self and in God.

Further Thought and Action

Reflection

We are a people who believe in communication, in making our-selves heard. Also, we need to hear in return words of wisdom, tenderness and encouragement that will help us in the daily living of our lives. Prayer provides that communication with the divine. Prayer places us in the presence of God, a God who has already called us by name. We can speak to God and God can in turn speak to us. Yes, there are formal prayers and rituals, but our own thoughts and words form the purest prayer of all.

Just Imagine...

...long before daybreak, without waking any of those traveling with him, Jesus quietly leaves the house and goes off alone. When we awake we miss him, and a group of us, Simon Peter, Andrew, John and I, goes to the low hills outside the town searching for the Lord. We find him in a quiet olive grove, eyes closed, hands out-stretched, his whole being absorbed in conversation with his Father. Seeing him, we feel hungry, and are drawn in some strange way to share this wonderful experience. Forgetting for a moment the needs of the day, even the people awaiting us back in the city, we fall on our knees at his feet. "Lord, teach us to how pray," I blurt out.

90

Believe in prayer and pray regularly.

Words to Ponder:

"Ask, and it will given to you; seek and you will find; knock and it will be opened."

Questions to Ponder:

✚ When has God intervened in my life because of prayer? How is it that God speaks back to me?

✚ What was the most unexpected answer to a prayer?

✚ What is my favorite place of prayer and my favorite way of praying?

A Prayer

"Dear Lord, I pray to you now so that I might be able to pray. That might seem like a foolish prayer, but I do want to be able to set before you the things that are in my heart. Sometimes I don't quite have the right words and it never seems like the right time. Help me not to be self-conscious or lazy, and let me come to you as I know you to be—understanding, compassionate, concerned about me. And let me hear your voice, too, Lord in whatever way you choose to speak to me."

If Not Yet Yours, Making This Secret Your Own

You want to be able to pray, but it is difficult to know how to begin, what to say. Go to a quiet place and begin simply with this: tell God something about yourself, your life, your concerns, your needs.

When you have finished, say your first name ("Karen...." "Bob....") as if it were the first word God was using in speaking back to you. And then listen.

Promise yourself that you will take five or ten minutes a day for the next week to pray. Each day, come to God with some small part of you or your life.

If It Already Is,
A Way to Deepen the Secret

Addressing God in prayer is such a necessary part of life, but it may be time for a new level of trust in your prayer life. Oftentimes, we do not allow God the opportunity to communicate with us. Try to allow a few moments after your prayers—wherever they be said, whatever their form—for a response. Very few of us will actually ever hear God speaking back, but in the mystery that is the relationship of God to human beings, there are wordless ways the divine is imparted to us.

Might this also be the time to begin seeing a spiritual director, a person with whom you can talk about your spiritual journey?

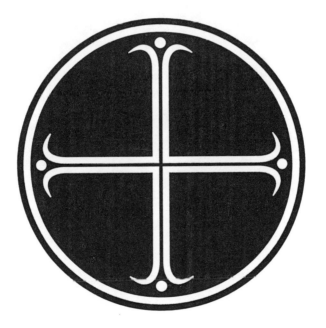

A Final Word

The Seven Secrets of Successful Catholics are interwoven, forming a sturdy yet flexible garment to wear through life. Such a garment will be rough or thin in spots, imperfect to be sure, yet, overall, it is easy to see the value and significance of these seemingly simple "secrets."

The Seven Secrets work. They are eminently practical. They are a combination of piety and practicality, common and divine sense, addressing both personal needs and those of the larger communities in which we are all a part. By living these secrets, Catholics are able to tap their native goodness and utilize their God-given creativity. They are able to have rich, full spiritual lives. They are able to be good people, citizens, parents, friends, workers, church members.

Successful Catholics are hardly perfect people, but they are the core of a new laity that is transforming the church and that has the potential to be the leaven to transform society. They are people who take seriously the call to greatness that the life of Christ represents and that our world so badly needs to see demonstrated.

Perhaps you have other secrets or variations on these seven that haven't been mentioned on these pages. Will you tell the rest of us about them, so we might weave them into our garments too? You can write to: Seven Secrets, Paulist Press, 997 Macarthur Blvd., Mahwah, N.J. 07430, or you can share your insights and learn those of others on a web site dedicated to those who are struggling to develop their own Catholic "habit of being." The electronic address is: http://www.bcinet.net/goodenuf/